Glendale Library, Arts & Culture Dept.

3 9 0 1 0 0 5 6 8 5 4 9 5 7

CHILDREN'S ROOM

S0-BTR-158

NO LONGER PROPERTY OF
GLENDALE LIBRARY,
ARTS & CULTURE DEPT.

Behind the Scenes
with Coders

VIDEO GAME DEVELOPER

Jonathan and
Mariel Bard

PowerKiDS
press.

New York

j 794.8153 BAR

Published in 2018 by The Rosen Publishing Group, Inc.
29 East 21st Street, New York, NY 10010

Copyright © 2018 by The Rosen Publishing Group, Inc.

All rights reserved. No part of this book may be reproduced in any form without permission in writing from the publisher, except by a reviewer.

First Edition

Editor: Melissa Raé Shofner
Book Design: Mickey Harmon
Interior Layout: Rachel Rising

Photo Credits: Cover, pp. 1, 3–32 (background) Lukas RS/Shutterstock.com; Cover Adam Vilimek/Shutterstock.com; Cover, p. 11 Syda Productions/Shutterstock.com; p. 5 Matic Stojs/Shutterstock.com; p. 6 stephen rudolph/Shutterstock.com; p. 7 f8 Imaging/Hulton Archive/Getty Images; p. 8 ©iStockphoto.com/daz2d; p. 9 Tinxi/Shutterstock.com; p. 10 Neveshkin Nikolay/Shutterstock.com; p. 13 wavebreakmedia/Shutterstock.com; p. 15 GaudiLab/Shutterstock.com; p. 17 WAYHOME studio/Shutterstock.com; p. 18 FabrikaSimf/Shutterstock.com; p. 19 Billion Photos/Shutterstock.com; p. 21 Now Design/Shutterstock.com; p. 23 Nejron Photo/Shutterstock.com; p. 25 ESB Professional/Shutterstock.com; p. 26 Sentavio/Shutterstock.com; p. 27 nullplus/Shutterstock.com; p. 29 g-stockstudio/Shutterstock.com; p. 30 ProStockStudio/Shutterstock.com.

Cataloging-in-Publication Data
Names: Bard, Jonathan.
Title: Video game developer / Jonathan and Mariel Bard.
Description: New York : PowerKids Press, 2018. | Series: Behind the scenes with coders | Includes index.
Identifiers: ISBN 9781508155744 (pbk.) | ISBN 9781508155683 (library bound) | ISBN 9781508155560 (6 pack)
Subjects: LCSH: Video games–Design–Vocational guidance–Juvenile literature. | Video games industry–Vocational guidance–Juvenile literature. | Computer games–Programming–Vocational guidance–Juvenile literature.
Classification: LCC QA76.76.C672 B37 2018 | DDC 794.8′1536–dc23

Manufactured in the United States of America

CPSIA Compliance Information: Batch ##BS17PK: For Further Information contact Rosen Publishing, New York, New York at 1-800-237-9932

Contents

A Coded World

From the time we wake up to the time we go to bed, we use all kinds of devices to make our lives easier. From small devices, such as smartphones, to large ones, such as airplanes, **technology** is important to us. What makes much of this technology possible is a hidden set of instructions called code. Code is similar to the steps of a recipe. There are many steps to a recipe, such as adding flour and sugar when making cookies. The programs that run our electronic devices have many lines of code. Each line of code tells a device to do something, such as turn on or play music.

Video games have code, too. Every action, including saving your progress and keeping track of high scores, requires coding by professional video game developers.

Every step in a cookie recipe adds up to a yummy result. Similarly, lines of code come together to create an awesome video game.

Early Code

The first computer programmer was a British mathematician named Ada Lovelace. In 1843, Lovelace wrote the first algorithm designed for a machine—even though there was no computer to run her program. An algorithm is a specific set of instructions—much like a recipe—to complete one task. In 1957, John Backus created the first high-level programming language. It was called FORTRAN.

We've come a long way since 1843. Programmers today code everything from simple text files to music and games. Video games in particular have changed from simple 2-D games to interactive 3-D worlds with millions of people playing at the same time. If we didn't have programmers coding each piece of game instruction for computers to use, video games wouldn't exist.

Early computers were gigantic! Some took up an entire room and required a ton of power to run.

Tech Talk

There's an entire programming language named for Ada Lovelace. It's called Ada and it was used by the U.S. Department of Defense. It was known for being really hard for **hackers** to mess with!

Early Video Games

Early video games were not as fancy or **complicated** as the ones we play today. At the time, though, they were a giant leap forward for technology. The first game designed purely for fun was *Tennis for Two*, programmed in 1958. It wasn't until 1962, with a game called *Spacewar!*, that the idea of video games really exploded.

Over the past 50 years, technology has become better and better. **Graphics** have improved, and computers have become much less expensive. In the late 1950s and 1960s, computers were far too expensive for average people to buy. That made it hard for anyone to enjoy the earliest games. It wasn't until computers and game systems became more affordable that video game development really took off as a career.

In 1972, Atari, an early video game company, released a very popular game called *Pong*. *Pong* was the first major success in the video game industry.

Arcade Games

It's hard to find classic **arcades** today, as most of them have sold their machines and closed down. When they first opened, however, pinball was the game of choice. From the 1930s to the 1970s, pinball arcades were very popular. Then along came video games. Early video games like *Pong* and *Space Invaders* quickly replaced pinball as the way to spend quarters. Video games were new, fun, and different— and they were easier to fix if something broke!

How Are Video Games Made?

All video games, whether on a computer, a tablet, or a smartphone, start with the same first step: a great idea! Behind those great ideas are game designers and game developers. Before any lines of code can be written, game designers have to figure out all the little details of a game's world. Much like authors, game designers take the time to create characters, a setting, and a story. They're also in charge of making the game's rules, such as how and when to award points.

Game developers take a designer's great ideas and turn them into video games we can play. Game developers lead teams of programmers who use their coding skills to make the final product.

Game designers have to think about all aspects of a game, from telling an interesting story to designing the game's controls. Game developers take these ideas and make them a reality.

Working as a Team

Once the designers have worked out their great ideas, game developers get ready to start programming a video game. Sound **engineers** need to find all the sound effects that will be programmed into the game. Sound makes a huge difference in a player's gaming experience. Take a baseball video game, for example. There are many sounds you might hear at a ballpark: the crack of a bat hitting a ball, the crowd cheering, or the umpire yelling, "Safe!" All of these sounds need to be ready for the programmers so they can make the game more lifelike.

At the same time, artists are designing the characters, writers are developing the story, and so on—all before anything is coded.

Tech Talk

When it comes to video games, "developer" can refer to a single person or a large company. The original *Minecraft* was developed by a single person, while *World of Warcraft* has over 4,000 people working on it!

No matter how many people are on the programming team, each person plays an important role in creating a great video game.

Rules and Goals

Have you ever played a video game where your character could jump? Game designers decided every element of that jump, including how high and how far the character could go. How do players score points? Which player goes first? How do characters interact with each other? These and other rules of the game are all decided before a game is coded.

This is also when designers decide the goal of the game. Is it to score the most points or to beat an opponent? Or is it to get to a certain place or find a specific item?

Planning out every detail, even the height and distance of a simple jump, is very important and a lot of fun! If the designer can dream it, there's a way for game developers to program it.

The rules of a game need to be reviewed carefully. If a game is too hard or too easy, it won't be fun to play.

Lead Programmers

Once the game designers are happy with the **concept** of a game, they send their ideas to experienced programmers on the developer team. These people are called lead programmers. Lead programmers specialize in translating game designers' visions into code. They're experts in their field and help other programmers on their team write the actual code for the games. Lead programmers are often **fluent** in many coding languages. Three popular coding languages for video games are C++ (pronounced "C plus plus"), Java, and C# (pronounced "C sharp").

Lead programmers focus on creating the game and keeping it on schedule. They decide how each line of code will be written and who will write it. They're also the ones who make sure all the code works together.

Communication with team members is very important to keeping big projects on track.

Lots of Languages

Some programming languages work better for certain projects than others. For science-related projects, C++ and Python are often used. In advertising, PHP, Java, and JavaScript might be better for the job. In many cases, a single product, website, or game will use multiple languages. The websites for companies such as Twitter, Amazon, and Google use JavaScript for what you see, but behind the scenes, programmers use a combination of other languages to create the finished products.

Graphics Programmers

By this point in game development, the designers have given the artists and graphics programmers their ideas about how they want the game to look and feel. Everything you see—from the start-up menu to the final boss battle—are created by artists and brought to life by graphics programmers.

One important tool many graphics programmers use is Visual Studio, which is a **software** program that lets them see how changing code will affect the appearance of an on-screen object. Graphics programmers work to make the game the best it can be whether it's played on a computer, tablet, or phone. They work very hard to give you a great gaming experience.

digital drawing tablet

Artists create digital copies of their artwork, which programmers then code into the game.

IDEs

Visual Studio is a software program that makes coding easier. It's an IDE, or integrated development environment. IDE software allows programmers to organize and share their work with teammates, find **bugs**, and visualize their code, all in one program. By putting all these tools together, it saves the programmer time and helps them be more productive. IDEs are such powerful, useful tools that almost all programmers use them.

User-Interface Programmers

When you play a video game, you see key pieces of information on the screen. In a racing game, you'll see a view of the track. You'll also often see a map of the route, your position compared to other players, your speed, and how much time has gone by. The game designers decided this was important information for you to see, so it's carefully planned and coded by a user-interface programmer.

An interface determines how you see and interact with the game, and a user-interface programmer works with the rest of the programming team to make sure you have all the in-game information you need. They also program the menus and options you might need to use in a game, such as "Save" to save your progress or "Quit" to stop playing.

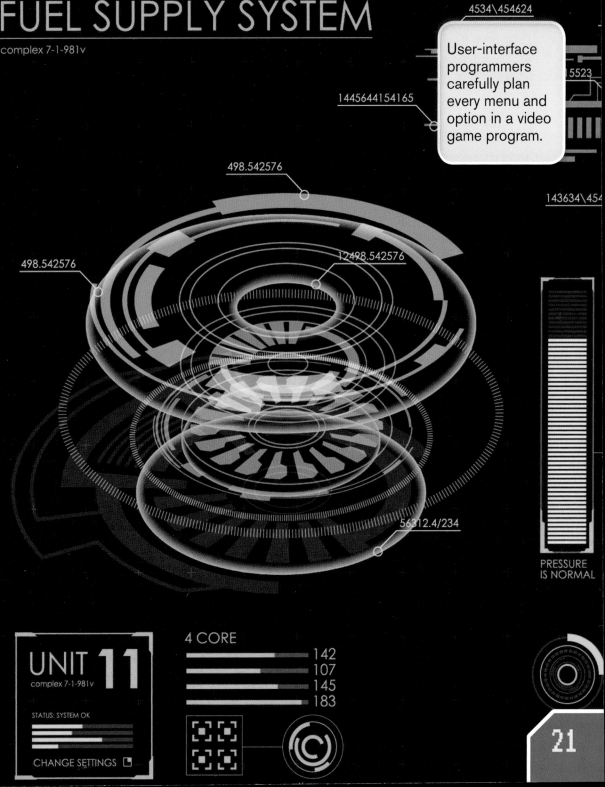

FUEL SUPPLY SYSTEM

complex 7-1-981v

User-interface programmers carefully plan every menu and option in a video game program.

Audio Programmers

Music and sound effects create a more complete gaming experience. Every time you interact in some way with the game, there is a sound to go with it. If you're running out of time to finish a puzzle, the game's background music likely speeds up to put the pressure on.

Sound effects in a game are carefully planned by sound engineers and added to the game by audio, or sound, programmers. Audio programmers also decide how far away something sounds. Is the noise close to you or off in the distance? Changing this can affect your game experience.

Most of the code written to control sound is in the same coding language as the rest of the game. A strong background in C++ is very helpful for audio programmers working on video games.

Mixing sounds and preparing them for coding is very **technical** and can be hard. However, it helps contribute to a great game that draws players in with its rich sounds and experiences.

Network Programmers

The Internet makes it easy to contact our friends through e-mail, social media, and video chat. People can also use the Internet to play video games with others around the world. In order to connect two players in different locations, **network** programmers write special code that lets the two devices "talk" to each other.

Network programmers connect gamers across the globe while making sure players' devices can communicate very quickly. They also have to make sure the connections are secure. No one wants to play a game where someone can cheat or hack them! Network programmers understand how information is sent over the Internet. They know how to write secure code to limit cheating. They use special computer protocols, or rules, called UDP (user datagram protocol) and TCP/IP (transmission control protocol/Internet protocol).

Connecting with friends to play video games online is easy. If you use a headset, you can talk to one person or a bunch of people at the same time.

Tech Talk ● ○ ○

Candy Crush is a popular game people play on their smartphones and tablets. The program has to support almost 100 million people logging in every day! That's a lot of information to handle for a single game.

Finding Bugs!

Once all the code is written, the lead programmer and their team make sure everything is working correctly. They check through all of a game's code for bugs. This can be hard and may take a long time. Extra people are often needed to look for mistakes. Programmers can write their own tests to check for bugs by guessing how players will interact with a game.

To reduce the number of bugs found at the end of game development, programmers can use a process called pair programming. This is when two people work at the same computer while developing code. One person writes the code, while the other makes sure it's written correctly. This can help find bugs much earlier in the process.

```
        m_fNS = (ro \ (1-ro)*((1-(ro/2));
        m_fNW = ro*ro \ (2*(1-ro));
        m_ftS = m_fNS\lambda;
        m_ftW = m_fNW\lambda;

97 ●     CalCPn(0.5f, ro, m_aPN);
98     }
99
100 int  void CalCMEk1(float Eta, float Etb,
101     }
102     float lambda = 1\Eta;
103     float mu = 1\Etb;
104     float ro = lambda\mu;
105     float kfloat = (float)k;
106     if(ro>1)
107     }
108     m_fNS = float.PositiveInfinity;
109     m_fNW = float.PositiveInfinity;
110     m_ftS = float.PositiveInfinity;
111     m_ftW = float.PositiveInfinity;
112     return;
113     }
114     m_fNS = (ro \ (1-ro)) * (1- (ro)*(kf
115     m_fNW = (lambda*lambda\(k*mu*mu) + r
116     m_ftS = m_fNS \ lambda;
117     m_ftW = ((kfloat+1) \ (2*kfloat)) * (
118
119     double s = (double)Etb\Math.Sqrt((do
120     double vb = (s*s) \ (Etb*Etb);
121     float v = 0.5f* (1+(float)vb);
122     CalCPn(v, ro, m_aPN);
123     }
```

Tracking down errors in code is difficult work that requires a lot of patience.

Tech Talk

In 1947, programmers working on a computer for the U.S. Navy found a moth stuck inside. It was a real-life computer bug! Luckily, the little critter didn't cause too much damage.

Releasing the Game

Before a game is released, the team of developers and designers takes time to play it. This is called alpha testing. When the designers and developers are satisfied, the game is usually released to a small number of people for **beta testing**. These players find any remaining bugs and report them to the developers, who make final coding changes to the game before it's available to everyone.

Depending on the type of game, programmers sometimes continue to create new levels after the game is released. They code changes and new features to keep the game updated so people keep playing. One of the most difficult programming jobs to do is coding changes that make the game better after it has been released—without adding new bugs.

Releasing a finished game to the world completes the video game development process.

Do You Want to Be a Game Developer?

Creating a video game takes a lot of work. The game development team is made up of many people, including graphics programmers, network programmers, and audio programmers. Even more people are needed to debug and test a new game. Each person adds a special skill to the team.

Creating and maintaining a video game involves a lot of coding. It isn't always easy, but working as a game developer can be a very rewarding career. Even though many players don't think about the work that goes into creating their favorite games, game developers still have the satisfaction of knowing they helped create a game enjoyed by thousands or even millions of people. One of the best parts of being a video game developer is getting to play the game yourself!

Glossary

arcade: A place where people play coin-operated games.

beta test: The testing of a product before release to the public, usually by testers from outside the developing company.

bug: An error in a line of code.

complicated: Difficult to explain or understand.

concept: A general idea.

engineer: Someone who plans and builds machines.

fluent: Able to speak or write another language easily and correctly.

graphic: A picture or shape.

hacker: Someone who uses a computer to gain unapproved access to data in a system, or a highly skilled computer expert.

network: A system of computers and databases that are all connected.

software: A program that runs on a computer and performs certain tasks.

technical: Of or relating to a mechanical or scientific subject.

technology: A method that uses science to solve problems and the tools used to solve those problems.

Index

Websites

Due to the changing nature of Internet links, PowerKids Press has developed an online list of websites related to the subject of this book. This site is updated regularly. Please use this link to access the list:
www.powerkidslinks.com/bsc/vgd